Safari Animals™

S0-CYG-238

MEERKATS

Katherine Walden

PowerKiDS press

New York

For Ali—friendly animals for my oldest friend

Published in 2009 by The Rosen Publishing Group, Inc.
29 East 21st Street, New York, NY 10010

First Edition

Editor: Amelie von Zumbusch
Book Design: Erica Clendening
Layout Design: Julio Gil
Photo Researcher: Jessica Gerweck

Photo Credits: All images Shutterstock.com.

Library of Congress Cataloging-in-Publication Data

Walden, Katherine.
  Meerkats / Katherine Walden. — 1st ed.
    p. cm. — (Safari animals)
  Includes index.
  ISBN 978-1-4358-2691-5 (library binding) — ISBN 978-1-4358-3065-3 (pbk.)
ISBN 978-1-4358-3077-6 (6-pack)
  1. Meerkat—Juvenile literature. I. Title.
  QL737.C235W35 2009
  599.74'2—dc22

                              2008020793

Manufactured in the United States of America

CONTENTS

This animal is a meerkat. Meerkats live on the hot, dry **plains** of southern Africa.

5

Meerkats have black fur around their eyes. This helps them see in the bright sunlight.

In the mornings, meerkats lie on their backs to warm up in the sunlight.

Meerkats live in groups of as many as 50 animals, called mobs. Mobs are also known as packs or gangs.

The meerkats in a mob live in the same burrow, or den. Each burrow has many **entrances**.

13

Meerkats dig in the ground for food. They eat bugs, small animals, and fruit.

While a mob gathers food, a few meerkats keep watch. These watchers call out when enemies come near.

Meerkats that are on watch often stand on their back legs. The meerkats use their tails to **balance** themselves.

Adult meerkats help keep all the babies in their mobs safe. Meerkat babies are called **pups**.

Meerkat pups play a lot. They also learn things, such as how to find food, from adult meerkats.

23

Words to Know

balance

entrance

plains

pup

Index

Web Sites

Due to the changing nature of Internet links, PowerKids Press has developed an online list of Web sites related to the subject of this book. This site is updated regularly. Please use this link to access the list:
www.powerkidslinks.com/safari/meerkat/